HELLO & CONTENTS

HELLO

Hello and welcome to Part 1 of No Head, No Hat, by Jenny and Tamzin. In this workbook, we are talking about the Hat - TEAMS! We are delighted to have you here. Let's get stuck in, we can't wait to support you. If you have any questions, please just email us tamzinjenny@gmail.com.

WHO ARE WE?

Meet our experts, Jenny Turner and Tamzin Hall, each bringing years of valuable experience to the table.

Jenny Turner spent over two decades at Hampshire County Council, progressing from a teacher to a Manager in the Primary Behaviour Service, excelling in team dynamics and support during challenging situations. Jenny is also a Thrive Trainer and Practitioner, emphasising the significance of relationships in learning and family connections.

Tamzin Hall boasts 20+ years in leadership, learning and development, and coaching, holding a BSc in Social Psychology and an Associate Certified Coach coaching qualification certified by the International Coaching Federation (ICF). Tamzin's dedication to psychology and personal development is evident through her active roles at the British Psychology Society and as an approved Mentor for the Association of Business Mentors.

We decided to set up NurturEd together because we believe that by combining our expertise, we can make a more significant impact than we ever could alone. Our collective experience and commitment to personal and professional development empower us to create positive change for individuals and organisations alike.

HELLO & CONTENTS

Introducing TEAMS CULTURE
by Nurtured Consultants

Today's school environment places increasing stress on our staff. Balancing student outcomes and managing behaviours that challenge is arduous, with growing exclusion rates and EHCP requests nationally. To support all schools in fostering inclusivity and resilience, we must first establish psychological safety for all staff. Without this, our educators cannot fully contribute.

Introducing TEAMS CULTURE, a framework to cultivate psychological safety in our schools. It's about realising tangible benefits for our school community. When staff feel safe, supported, and valued, they are empowered to give their best. This leads to improved student outcomes, reduced challenging behaviours, and a more positive school experience. TEAMS CULTURE aims to make our schools a place where every staff member can thrive and contribute effectively to our mission.

HELLO & CONTENTS

Contents
we are delighted you are here

0   HELLO & CONTENTS

1   SAFETY

2   MIND

3   ACCEPTED

4   EMPOWER

5   THRIVE

6   NEXT STEPS

When you believe in you, everyone else believes in you

— Marisa Peer

Chapter 1: Safety

No Head, No Hat

SAFETY

Ensuring that teachers feel safe within the school environment is crucial for the well-being and success of all stakeholders involved. When teachers feel psychologically safe, it directly benefits children, educators, and the individual teacher. A psychologically safe environment fosters open communication, trust, and collaboration among teachers, creating a more harmonious work atmosphere. This, in turn, positively impacts students, as they are more likely to thrive in a learning environment characterised by stability and support. Teachers who feel safe are better equipped to manage stress, exhibit mental toughness, and serve as role models for their students, emphasising the importance of resilience and self-confidence.

> **Write down any thoughts or ideas on how you can incorporate this into your school.**
>
> Write your answer here...

Individually, a sense of safety enhances job satisfaction, reduces burnout, and promotes a long-lasting commitment to the teaching profession.

Chapter 1:
Safety

No Head, No Hat

What does it mean for your teachers to feel safe?

Creating psychological safety for teachers involves fostering an environment where they can freely express ideas, concerns, and innovations without fear. This builds trust and open communication, enabling collaboration and improvement. This empowerment leads to a dynamic teaching workforce that adapts, experiments, and confidently faces challenges, benefiting student learning.

N.1
Teacher Well-Being

Teachers who feel safe experience lower levels of stress, anxiety, and burnout. This contributes to their overall well-being, which, in turn, positively impacts their job satisfaction and effectiveness.

N.2
Retention & Recruitment

Schools with a safe and supportive atmosphere are more likely to retain experienced teachers and attract new, high-quality educators. This can lead to greater continuity and stability in the teaching staff.

N.3
Effective Teaching & Learning

A safe environment enables teachers to concentrate on teaching. When they feel secure, they can invest more energy in planning lessons and helping students, resulting in better learning outcomes.

N.4
Collaboration and Professional Growth

Teacher safety fosters a sense of trust and collaboration among educators. They are more likely to work together, share best practices, and engage in professional development opportunities, which can enhance teaching quality and innovation.

Chapter 1: Safety

No Head, No Hat

N.5
Positive School Culture

A safe environment contributes to a positive school culture. This culture promotes a sense of belonging, respect, and cooperation among all members of the school community — teachers, students, parents, and administrators.

N.6
Student Well-Being

Teachers who feel safe are better equipped to create a supportive classroom environment. This positively impacts students' emotional well-being, as they are more likely to feel secure and valued.

N.7
Innovation and Creativity

Safe environments encourage teachers to be innovative and creative in their teaching methods. They are more likely to experiment with new approaches and technologies, leading to more engaging and effective teaching.

N.8
Teacher-Student Relationships

Feeling safe allows teachers to build stronger, more trusting relationships with their students. These relationships are essential for effective teaching and for providing emotional support to students.

N.9
Reduced Turnover Costs

High teacher turnover can be costly for schools in terms of recruitment, training, and the disruption it causes. When teachers feel safe, turnover rates tend to be lower, saving the school resources and maintaining stability.

Ultimately, when teachers feel and are safe, it creates a domino effect of positivity that enhances the educational journey for all involved, contributing to a healthier, more productive, and thriving school community.

Chapter 1:
Safety

NOTES

No Head, No Hat

How does your school enable you to feel SAFE?

Write your answer here...

What do you need to feel SAFER? – inside & outside of school.

Write your answer here...

Chapter 1:
Safety

No Head, No Hat

Five tips to help teachers to feel safe in school

Open and Supportive Communication: Foster a culture of open and supportive communication where school leaders actively listen to teachers' concerns, ideas, and feedback without judgement. Encourage honest dialogue and ensure that teachers feel their voices are heard and valued.

Write your thoughts/notes here...

Clear Expectations and Guidelines: Establish clear expectations and guidelines for behaviour and performance within the school community. When everyone understands the standards, it reduces ambiguity and promotes a sense of psychological safety.

Write your thoughts/notes here...

Professional Development and Training: Offer training that equips teachers with the skills they need to excel. This boosts their confidence and psychological safety.

Write your thoughts/notes here...

Chapter 1: Safety

No Head, No Hat

Recognition and Appreciation: Celebrating teachers' achievements and milestones, whether through awards, acknowledgments, or simple gestures of appreciation, boosts their morale and reinforces their commitment to their profession.

Write your thoughts/notes here...

Conflict Resolution Mechanisms: Implement effective conflict resolution mechanisms that allow teachers to address and resolve issues or conflicts in a fair and constructive manner. Knowing there are processes in place to address concerns can enhance feelings of safety.

Write your thoughts/notes here...

Chapter 1: Safety

No Head, No Hat

Exercise

"Cultivating Psychological Safety"

N.1 - SELF REFLECTION

1. Find a quiet and comfortable space to work on this exercise alone.
2. Take a few minutes to centre yourself and focus on the task.
3. In the workbook, create a two-column table with the headings "Cultivating Psychological Safety" and "Action Steps."

N.2 - IDENTIFYING WAYS TO CULTIVATE PSYCHOLOGICAL SAFETY

1. In the "Cultivating Psychological Safety" column, list specific ways in which you, as a school head or teacher, can contribute to fostering an environment of psychological safety. These could include actions like active listening, empathy, clear communication, or providing opportunities for feedback.
2. For each idea you list, briefly explain why it is important and how it can contribute to a more psychologically safe culture.

N.3 - SETTING ACTION STEPS

1. In the "Action Steps" column, next to each idea, write down one or more specific actions you can take to put these ideas into practice within your role.
2. Be practical and realistic in your action steps. These should be actions you can initiate independently or with minimal support.

Chapter 1: Safety

No Head, No Hat

Exercise continued....

"Cultivating Psychological Safety"

N4 - PRIORITISE AND COMMIT

1. Review your list of ideas and action steps. Identify the top two or three areas you'd like to prioritise for immediate implementation.
2. Circle or highlight the chosen action steps and commit to working on them in the coming weeks or months.

N.5 - SUMMARY

1. Summarise the exercise by writing a brief paragraph in your workbook. Reflect on how completing this exercise has deepened your understanding of your role in fostering psychological safety within the school community.

Chapter 1:
Safety

No Head, No Hat

Exercise cont....

"Cultivating Psychological Safety"

This exercise is designed for school heads and teachers to reflect on their roles in fostering psychological safety within the school community and to set personal goals for creating an environment where all feel safe to express themselves and take risks.

Your thoughts & notes, reflections and ideas

"People will trust their leaders when their leaders do the things that make them feel psychologically safe"

Simon Sinek

Chapter 1: Safety

No Head, No Hat

Your thoughts & notes, reflections and ideas continued...

It is important for teachers to feel safe because a sense of safety fosters a supportive and productive educational environment, enabling open communication, risk-taking, and a culture of continuous improvement that benefits both educators and students.

Chapter 2:
Mind

No Head, No Hat

Being held in mind and listened to is essential for the well-being and growth of teachers and school staff. Recognising and respecting the unique needs of individuals is a cornerstone of creating a supportive environment. By implementing processes that allow for open discussions, we ensure that due consideration is given to each staff member. This approach fosters a sense of inclusivity, where everyone feels valued and their concerns are heard. When teachers are kept in mind, they experience a greater sense of belonging and psychological safety, which, in turn, enables them to provide more effective support to their students. This supportive atmosphere not only enhances teacher job satisfaction and reduces burnout but also has a profound impact on children's learning experiences.

> Write down any thoughts or ideas on how you can incorporate this into your school.
>
> Write your answer here...

By cultivating a culture of psychological safety and acceptance for teachers, we create a harmonious and empowering educational ecosystem that benefits everyone involved.

Chapter 2: Mind

No Head, No Hat

What does mind mean for the teachers in your school?

Students benefit from an educational environment where teachers are empowered and accepted, and their unique needs are taken into account, as it leads to more engaging, empathetic, and effective teaching practices. Ultimately, keeping teachers in mind and ensuring their well-being contributes to a harmonious and thriving educational community.

N.1 Frequent Communication

Establish open and frequent lines of communication with teachers. Encourage them to share their thoughts, concerns, and suggestions regularly.

N.2 Feedback Loops

Create feedback mechanisms, such as surveys or suggestion boxes, where teachers can provide anonymous feedback if they wish, ensuring their voices are heard.

N.3 Professional Development Support

Provide resources and support for teachers to pursue professional development opportunities that align with their career goals and interests.

N.4 Recognition and Appreciation

Recognise and celebrate teachers' accomplishments through awards, recognition events, or simple gestures of appreciation.

Chapter 2: Mind

N.5
Inclusive Decision-Making

Involve teachers in decision-making processes related to curriculum, school policies, and resource allocation, valuing their input and expertise.

N.6
Flexible Work Arrangements

Offer flexible work arrangements, when possible, to accommodate teachers' personal needs and work-life balance.

N.7
Wellness Programmes

Implement wellness programmes that address teachers' physical and mental well-being, providing access to counselling services, stress management workshops, and wellness activities.

N.8
Professional Growth Opportunities

Encourage teachers to pursue advanced degrees, certifications, or additional training by providing support and recognising their achievements.

N.9
Constructive Conflict Resolution

Establish effective conflict resolution mechanisms that allow teachers to address and resolve issues in a fair and constructive manner.

For a school, keeping teachers in mind means acknowledging their importance and recognising the pivotal role they play in the educational process. It signifies creating an environment where teachers' needs, concerns, and professional growth are prioritised.

Chapter 2:
Mind

No Head, No Hat

NOTES

How does your school enable you to feel kept in MIND?

Write your answer here...

What do you need to feel more kept in MIND? – inside & outside of school.

Write your answer here...

Chapter 2:
Mind

No Head, No Hat

Five tips to help teachers feel kept in mind in school

Regular Communication: Open and regular communication channels between teachers and school administration foster a sense of being heard and valued. When teachers can voice their concerns, share ideas, and provide feedback, it leads to a more collaborative and positive school environment.

Write your thoughts/notes here...

Mental Health and Well-Being Support: Recognising and addressing the mental health and well-being of teachers is crucial. Providing access to counselling services, stress management programmes, coaches, and work-life balance initiatives helps prevent burnout and maintains teacher morale.

Write your thoughts/notes here...

Involvement in Decision-Making: Including teachers in the decision-making processes that affect their work and students can lead to better, more informed choices. Teachers often have valuable insights into what works best in the classroom.

Write your thoughts/notes here...

**Chapter 2:
Mind**

No Head, No Hat

Recognition and Appreciation: Celebrating teachers' achievements and milestones, whether through awards, acknowledgments, or simple gestures of appreciation, boosts their morale and reinforces their commitment to their profession.

Write your thoughts/notes here...

Flexible Teaching Approaches: Recognizing that teachers have diverse strengths and teaching styles and allowing them flexibility in how they deliver lessons empowers them. This flexibility can lead to more engaging and effective instruction tailored to the needs of their students.

Write your thoughts/notes here...

Chapter 2:
Mind

No Head, No Hat

Exercise

"Cultivating a Culture of Keeping Teachers in Mind"

N.1 - SELF REFLECTION

1. Find a quiet and comfortable space to work on this exercise alone.
2. Take a few minutes to centre yourself and focus on the task.
3. In the workbook, create a two-column table with the headings "Cultivating a Culture" and "Action Steps."

N.2 - IDENTIFYING WAYS TO CULTIVATE A CULTURE

1. In the "Cultivating a Culture" column, list specific ways in which you, as a school head or teacher, can contribute to fostering a culture that prioritises keeping teachers in mind. These could include actions like promoting open communication, recognising achievements, providing professional development opportunities, or supporting work-life balance.
2. For each idea you list, briefly explain why it is important and how it can contribute to a more teacher-centered culture.

N.3 - SETTING ACTION STEPS

1. In the "Action Steps" column, next to each idea, write down one or more specific actions you can take to put these ideas into practice within your role.
2. Be practical and realistic in your action steps. These should be actions you can initiate independently or with minimal support.

Chapter 2:
Mind

No Head, No Hat

Exercise continued....

"Cultivating a Culture of Keeping Teachers in Mind"

N4 - PRIORITISE AND COMMIT

1. Review your list of ideas and action steps. Identify the top two or three areas you'd like to prioritise for immediate implementation.
2. Circle or highlight the chosen action steps and commit to working on them in the coming weeks or months.

N.5 - SUMMARY

1. Summarise the exercise by writing a brief paragraph in your workbook. Reflect on how completing this exercise has deepened your understanding of your role in cultivating a culture that keeps teachers in mind.

Chapter 2: Mind

No Head, No Hat

Exercise cont....

"Cultivating a Culture of Keeping Teachers in Mind"

This exercise is designed for school heads and teachers to reflect on their roles in fostering a culture that prioritises the well-being and growth of educators, and to set personal goals for creating an environment where teachers feel valued and heard.

Your thoughts & notes, reflections and ideas

"A little consideration, a little thought for others makes all the difference"

Chapter 2: Mind

No Head, No Hat

Your thoughts & notes, reflections and ideas continued…

It is crucial to keep teachers in mind because prioritising their well-being and growth creates a supportive and empowered educational environment, ultimately leading to improved teaching quality and student outcomes.

Chapter 3: Accepted

Accepted

It is crucial for teachers to feel accepted and valued in their roles as educators, as this acceptance has profound effects on children, the teachers themselves, and individuals within the educational community. When teachers feel accepted, they create a positive and inclusive learning environment where students can flourish emotionally and academically. Acceptance fosters strong teacher-student relationships built on trust and mutual respect, enabling effective communication and support for students' social-emotional development. When teachers experience acceptance within their professional community, they are more likely to exhibit mental toughness and resilience, setting a valuable example for students. They become better equipped to handle the challenges of teaching, ultimately reducing burnout and promoting a more nurturing atmosphere. At an individual level, acceptance of teachers enhances their job satisfaction, motivation, and overall well-being, contributing to a stable and dedicated teaching workforce.

Write down any thoughts or ideas on how you can incorporate this into your school.

Write your answer here...

By cultivating a culture of psychological safety and acceptance for teachers, we create a harmonious and empowering educational ecosystem that benefits everyone involved.

Chapter 3:
Accepted

No Head, No Hat

What does acceptance mean for the teachers in your school?

Fostering an accepting culture for our teachers means creating an environment where they feel respected, supported, and valued for their contributions. This involves recognising their diverse strengths, experiences, and perspectives. In such a culture, teachers can freely express ideas, share challenges, and collaborate without fear of judgment.

N.1 Acceptance of Diversity

Teachers of diverse backgrounds, abilities, and learning styles are accepted and valued, including differences in race, ethnicity, gender, religion, socio-economic status, and more. Schools must promote inclusivity and prevent discrimination or marginalization.

N.2 Acceptance of Individuality

Each teacher and student is unique, with strengths and weaknesses. Accepting and appreciating these differences is crucial, allowing for adaptations to accommodate diverse learning styles and recognizing that not everyone excels in the same way or at the same pace.

N.3 Acceptance of Mistakes

Schools need to be a safe space for staff and students to make mistakes and learn from them. They should encourage a growth mindset, where everyone understands that making errors is a natural part of the learning process.

N.4 Acceptance of Questions

Staff and students should be encouraged to ask questions and seek clarification when they don't understand something. Schools should create an atmosphere where everyone feels accepted and comfortable asking questions without fear of judgment.

Chapter 3: Accepted

N.5
Acceptance of Responsibility

Teachers need to be accountable for the quality of their teaching, the content they deliver, and the impact they have on their students' lives whilst being supported appropriately and empathetically. It also involves accepting the need for continuous professional development to further develop skills.

N.6
Acceptance of Individual Goals

Recognising that each teacher and student may have different goals and aspirations is important. Schools should help everyone to set and work towards their individual academic and personal goals, accepting that these goals may vary from one person to another.

Acceptance also refers to the principles, beliefs, and practices that promote inclusivity, diversity, and a welcoming environment within the school community. Here's what acceptance and associated values can entail for a school.

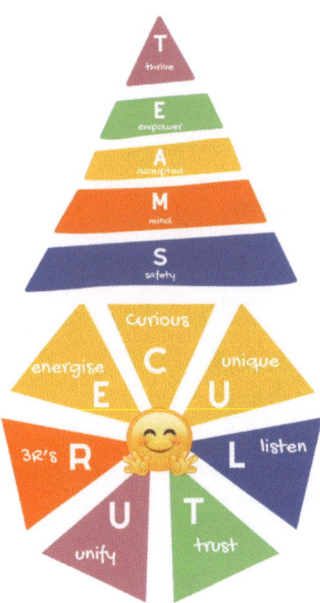

Chapter 3:
Accepted

NOTES

No Head, No Hat

How does your school enable you to feel ACCECPTED?

Write your answer here...

What do you need to feel more ACCECPTED? - inside & outside of school.

Write your answer here...

Chapter 3: Accepted

Five tips to help teachers feel accepted in school

Open and Respectful Communication: Encourage open and respectful communication among teachers, school leadership, and staff. Create spaces for idea sharing, addressing concerns, and sharing experiences without fear of judgment. Ensure feedback remains constructive and supportive.

Write your thoughts/notes here…

Professional Development and Growth Invest in ongoing professional development for teachers to enhance skills and stay updated. Allocate resources for them to attend relevant workshops, conferences, and training sessions that align with their interests and goals.

Write your thoughts/notes here…

Mentoring and Peer Support: Establish mentoring and peer support networks in the school. Experienced teachers can mentor newer colleagues, fostering guidance and community. Peer collaboration promotes acceptance and a sense of belonging.

Write your thoughts/notes here…

Chapter 3:
Accepted

No Head, No Hat

Recognition and Appreciation: Regularly recognise and appreciate the efforts of teachers. Celebrate their achievements, both big and small, in staff meetings, newsletters, or through awards. Acknowledging their contributions reinforces their value within the school community.

Write your thoughts/notes here...

Inclusive Policies and Practices: Implement policies and practices that promote inclusivity and diversity within the school. Ensure that all staff members, regardless of their background, feel included and respected. Address any issues of bias or discrimination promptly and effectively.

Write your thoughts/notes here...

Chapter 3: Accepted

No Head, No Hat

Exercise

"Building a Culture of Acceptance"

N.1 - SELF REFLECTION

1. Find a quiet and comfortable space to work on this exercise alone.
2. Take a few minutes to centre yourself and focus on the task.
3. In the workbook, create a two-column table with the headings "Promoting Acceptance" and "Action Steps."

N.2 - IDENTIFYING WAYS TO PROMOTE ACCEPTANCE

1. In the "Promoting Acceptance" column, list specific ways in which you, as a school head or teacher, can contribute to creating a culture of acceptance within your school community. These could include actions like leading by example, fostering diversity and inclusion, promoting empathy, or addressing conflicts constructively.
2. For each idea you list, briefly explain why it is important and how it can contribute to a more accepting school environment.

N.3 - SETTING ACTION STEPS

1. In the "Action Steps" column, next to each idea, write down one or more specific actions you can take to put these ideas into practice within your role.
2. Be practical and realistic in your action steps. These should be actions you can initiate independently or with minimal support.

Chapter 3:
Accepted

No Head, No Hat

Exercise continued....

"Building a Culture of Acceptance"

N4 - PRIORITISE AND COMMIT

1. Review your list of ideas and action steps. Identify the top two or three areas you'd like to prioritise for immediate implementation.
2. Circle or highlight the chosen action steps and commit to working on them in the coming weeks or months.

N.5 - SUMMARY

1. Summarise the exercise by writing a brief paragraph in your workbook. Reflect on how completing this exercise has deepened your understanding of your role in fostering acceptance within the school community.

Chapter 3: Accepted

No Head, No Hat

Exercise cont....

"Building a Culture of Acceptance"

This exercise is designed for school heads and teachers to reflect on their roles in promoting a culture of acceptance within their school community and to set personal goals for fostering acceptance.

Your thoughts & notes, reflections and ideas

"Acceptance doesn't mean resignation: it means understanding that something is what it is and that there's got to be a way through it"

Michael J Fox

Chapter 3: Accepted

No Head, No Hat

Your thoughts & notes, reflections and ideas continued...

Creating a culture of acceptance involves nurturing an environment where teachers feel heard, valued, and empowered. When teachers feel accepted, they are more likely to be motivated, engaged, and committed to providing the best possible education for their students.

Chapter 4:
Empower

No Head, No Hat

Empower

When teachers are empowered, they possess the autonomy and confidence to innovate, adapt, and tailor their teaching methods to better meet the diverse needs of their students. This empowerment, in turn, creates a culture of collaboration and continuous improvement within schools. Students benefit greatly from such an environment, as it fosters engaging and personalised learning experiences that can ignite their passion for education. Furthermore, empowered teachers are more likely to effectively manage disruptive behaviours by utilising creative and empathetic strategies, ultimately enhancing classroom harmony. Importantly, teacher empowerment reduces stress levels, enhances job satisfaction, and promotes long-term retention in the profession, ensuring a stable and experienced teaching workforce.

Write down any thoughts or ideas on how you can incorporate this into your school.

Write your answer here...

The empowerment of teachers generates a positive cycle of growth and well-being that reverberates throughout the entire education ecosystem, benefiting children, educators, and society as a whole.

Chapter 4:
Empower

No Head, No Hat

What does it mean for your school when your teachers are empowered?

Empowering our teachers means providing them with the tools, support, and autonomy they need to excel in their roles. This has significant implications for schools:

N.1
Improved Learning Outcomes

Empowered teachers use innovative methods, improving student outcomes by tailoring approaches to diverse needs, creating an engaging learning environment.

N.2
Positive School Culture

When teachers feel empowered, it contributes to a positive school culture. They become more motivated, enthusiastic, and engaged in their work, which can inspire their colleagues and create a more collaborative and supportive atmosphere within the school.

N.3
Higher Retention

Empowered teachers tend to stay in their profession longer. They are less likely to experience burnout and are more satisfied with their careers. This leads to higher teacher retention rates, which are essential for maintaining continuity and stability within a school.

N.4
Professional Development

Empowered teachers are more likely to seek out and engage in ongoing professional development. They take the initiative to improve their skills and knowledge, which benefits not only them but also the entire school community.

Chapter 4:
Empower

No Head, No Hat

N.5
Enhanced School Reputation

Schools with empowered teachers often have a better reputation in the community. Positive word-of-mouth and the perception of a school as a place where educators are supported and encouraged can lead to increased enrolment and community support.

N.6
Innovation and Adaptability

Empowered teachers are more likely to embrace educational innovation and adapt to changes in the field. This ensures that the school remains dynamic and responsive to evolving educational needs and trends.

N.7
Student Engagement and Well-being

Empowered teachers are better equipped to address the needs of their students. They can create a safe and supportive classroom environment, which is essential for student well-being and engagement in the learning process.

Empowering teachers is not only beneficial for educators themselves but also has a profound impact on the overall functioning and success of schools. It leads to better educational outcomes, a positive school culture, and greater retention of experienced professionals, ultimately contributing to the long-term growth and reputation of the institution.

Chapter 4:
Empower

NOTES

No Head, No Hat

How does your school enable you to feel EMPOWERED?

Write your answer here...

What do you need to feel more EMPOWERED? – inside & outside of school.

Write your answer here...

Chapter 4: Empower

No Head, No Hat

Five tips to make teachers feel empowered in school

Professional Development Opportunities; Offer continuous professional development for teachers to enhance skills and stay updated with relevant trends through workshops, conferences, and training aligned with their goals and interests.

Write your thoughts/notes here...

Mentoring and Peer Support: Create mentoring and peer support networks in the school. Experienced teachers can mentor newer colleagues, fostering professional growth and a sense of community.

Write your thoughts/notes here...

Recognition and Feedback: Regularly appreciate teachers' efforts with constructive feedback on strengths and areas to improve, fostering motivation and a sense of accomplishment.

Write your thoughts/notes here...

Chapter 4:
Empower

No Head, No Hat

Flexibility in Work Arrangements: Provide flexible work options like part-time, job-sharing, or remote teaching to help teachers balance personal and professional lives, reducing stress and improving job satisfaction.

Write your thoughts/notes here…

Wellness Programmes: Implement wellness programmes and initiatives that prioritise teachers' physical and mental well-being. This can include access to coaching, mentoring or counselling services, stress management workshops, and initiatives that promote a healthy work-life balance.

Write your thoughts/notes here…

Chapter 4: Empower

No Head, No Hat

Exercise

"Empowerment Reflection and Sharing"

N.1 - SELF REFLECTION

1. Find a quiet and comfortable space to work on this exercise alone.
2. Take a few minutes to centre yourself and focus on the task.
3. In the workbook, create a two-column table with the headings "Empowering Factors" and "Action Steps."

N.2 - IDENTIFYING EMPOWERING FACTORS

1. In the "Empowering Factors" column, list the aspects of your role or your school's environment that contribute to your sense of empowerment. These could include factors like autonomy in decision-making, professional development opportunities, supportive leadership, or a positive work culture.
2. For each factor you list, briefly write down why it empowers you or enhances your job satisfaction. Reflect on specific experiences or situations that highlight these factors.

N.3 - SETTING ACTION STEPS

1. In the "Action Steps" column, next to each empowering factor, write down one or more specific actions or changes you can make to further empower yourself in that area.
2. Be practical and realistic in your action steps. These should be actions you can take on your own or with minimal support.

Chapter 4: Empower

No Head, No Hat

Exercise continued....

"Empowerment Reflection and Sharing"

N.4 - SHARING WITH A COLLEAGUE

1. Choose a trusted work colleague (e.g., another teacher, department head, or mentor) with whom you can share your reflections.
2. Schedule a brief meeting or conversation to discuss your empowerment reflections and action steps. Share your workbook or a summary of your findings.

N.5 - PRIORITISE AND COMMIT

1. Review your list of empowering factors and action steps, and consider any insights or feedback provided by your colleague.
2. Together with your colleague, identify which areas to prioritise for immediate improvement. Discuss the feasibility of your action steps and refine them if necessary.

N.6 - SUMMARY

1. Summarise the exercise by writing your thoughts on the next page. Reflect on how completing this exercise and discussing it with a colleague has enriched your understanding of empowerment in your role.

Chapter 4:
Empower

No Head, No Hat

Exercise cont....

"Empowerment Reflection and Sharing"

This exercise is designed for school heads and teachers to reflect on their roles, identify areas where they can feel more empowered, set personal goals for improvement, and engage in a meaningful discussion with a work colleague

Your thoughts & notes, reflections and ideas

"Change by its very nature is threatening, but it is also often productive."

Betty Ford

Chapter 4: Empower

Your thoughts & notes, reflections and ideas continued...

Empowering teachers is important because it leads to more effective and engaged educators, resulting in improved student learning outcomes, enhanced school culture, and a more dynamic and responsive education system.

Chapter 5:
Thrive

No Head, No Hat

THRIVE

It's crucial for teachers to thrive because their well-being has a profound impact on various levels. Firstly, thriving teachers positively influence the students they teach. When teachers are motivated, engaged, and passionate about their work, they inspire students to become lifelong learners and active participants in their education. This fosters a culture of excellence in schools, leading to improved student outcomes and a nurturing learning environment. Teacher well-being is also vital for their personal growth and satisfaction. Thriving educators experience reduced stress, better mental and physical health, and higher job satisfaction, enabling them to stay in the profession longer, ensuring a stable and experienced workforce in education.

Write down any thoughts or ideas on how you can incorporate this into your school.

Write your answer here...

Thriving teachers address disruptive behaviors by creating a supportive classroom atmosphere and guiding challenging students with empathy, reducing incidents and fostering a harmonious learning environment.

Chapter 5:
Thrive

No Head, No Hat

What does it means for your school when your teachers are thriving?

When teachers thrive, it empowers the school to cultivate a vibrant, nurturing learning environment that enhances both student success and the school's reputation. This has several positive implications for the school environment and the educational experience of students:

N.1
Improved Teaching Quality

Thriving teachers are more likely to be motivated, enthusiastic, and passionate about their work. This enthusiasm often translates into more engaging and effective teaching methods, leading to improved learning outcomes for students.

N.2
Positive School Culture

Thriving teachers enhance school culture by fostering collaboration, sharing ideas, and creating a supportive atmosphere, positively impacting relationships among staff and students.

N.3
Retention

Schools with thriving teachers tend to retain experienced and effective educators, preserving continuity and enhancing students' educational experiences. Thriving teachers staying in their roles provide stability to the school.

N.4
Innovation and Professional Development

Thriving teachers are often more open to innovation and continuous improvement. They may be more willing to explore new teaching methods, integrate technology, and participate in professional development opportunities, which can benefit both them and their students.

Chapter 5: Thrive

N.5
Student Engagement

Thriving teachers tend to be more attuned to their students' needs and interests. They can create a classroom environment that fosters student engagement, leading to better behavior and a more positive attitude toward learning.

N.6
Better Mental and Emotional Well-being

When teachers are thriving, they are less likely to experience burnout and stress. This not only benefits their own mental and emotional well-being but also ensures that they are available and emotionally present for their students.

N.7
Higher Student Achievement

Research has shown that student achievement is positively correlated with teacher well-being. When teachers are thriving, they are better equipped to support their students' academic growth and personal development.

N.8
Parent and Community Satisfaction

A school with thriving teachers often gathers more positive feedback from parents and the community. Satisfied teachers are more likely to communicate effectively with parents, leading to stronger partnerships between the school and families.

Chapter 5:
Thrive

No Head, No Hat

NOTES

How does your school enable you to THRIVE?

Write your answer here...

What else do you need to THRiVE more – inside & outside of school.

Write your answer here...

Chapter 5:
Thrive

No Head, No Hat

Five tips to help teachers thrive in school

Self-Care Routine; Prioritise self-care by maintaining a healthy work-life balance, getting enough rest, and engaging in activities that rejuvenate your mind and body.

Write your thoughts/notes here...

Continuous Professional Development: Keep up with professional development for classroom effectiveness through ongoing learning in teaching methods and technologies

Write your thoughts/notes here...

Support Network: Build a strong support network of colleagues, mentors, and friends who can provide guidance, share experiences, and offer emotional support during challenging times.

Write your thoughts/notes here...

Chapter 5:
Thrive

No Head, No Hat

Goal Setting: Set achievable goals for yourself, both personally and professionally, to stay motivated and focused on your growth as an educator.

Write your thoughts/notes here…

Reflect and Adapt: Reflect on your teaching, adapt to student needs, and embrace feedback for continuous improvement and a growth mindset.

Write your thoughts/notes here…

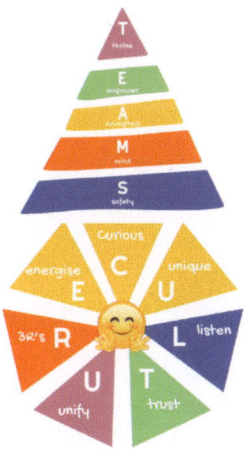

Chapter 5:
Thrive

 Exercise

"Daily Gratitude Journal"

N.1

Use the following pages: we are going to create a daily gratitude journal.

N.2

Set a Routine: Dedicate a few minutes each day, perhaps in the morning or before bed, to reflect on positive aspects of your teaching day.

N.3

Find your favourite spot, like a coffee shop or a cosy chair, close the door, and take 10 minutes for yourself. Bring your favorite drink and play music if you wish.

N.4

Write Three Things: Write down three things you're grateful for in your role as a teacher. These could be moments of student progress, supportive colleagues, a successful lesson, or any small victories.

N.5

Reflect and Smile: As you jot down these moments, take a moment to savour the positive emotions they bring. Reflect on how they make you feel.

N.6

Stay Consistent: Commit to this daily practice for a few weeks or more. Over time, it can help shift your focus towards the positive aspects of your teaching journey.

Chapter 5:
Thrive

No Head, No Hat

Exercise cont....

"Daily Gratitude Journal"

This simple exercise helps teachers thrive by fostering a more positive and resilient mindset, even during tough times. It reminds educators of the rewarding moments in their work, which can be a source of motivation and resilience.

Your thoughts & notes, reflections and ideas

"You are meant to THRIVE, not just SURVIVE"

Chapter 5: Thrive

No Head, No Hat

Your thoughts & notes, reflections and ideas continued...

Don't forget - It is important for our teachers to thrive because their well-being and professional fulfilment directly impact the quality of education they provide to students.

Chapter 6:
Next Steps

Next Steps

Congratulations on finishing this comprehensive ebook workbook designed for aspiring online content creators within our TEAMS CULTURE framework! Along this journey, you've acquired valuable insights, practical skills, and a strategic mindset to excel in the ever-evolving realm of online content creation.

Stay true to your passions, values, and personal brand

Thank you for working your way through this workbook. We appreciate the time and effort you've put into dedicating yourself to it. What insights have you gained? How do you plan to approach things differently moving forward?

What is the first thing you are going to do now? How can we helo you?

We believe in you, we celebrate you - and we can't wait to see all you achieve in the future.

Best of luck!

Jenny & Tamzin

Ps we would love to hear your thoughts on this workbook, please email us tamzinjenny@gmail.com

Pps we have a discount for you on Part 2 of No Head, No Hat. Email us to claim your discount tamzinjenny@gmail.com.

Want to work with us further? Let's chat - send us an email. We can't wait to hear from you.

Chapter 6:
Next Steps

We'd love to hear from you & support you in the future.

email us at
tamzinjenny@gmail.com
or visit our website
nurturedconsultants.co.uk

Jenny & Tamzin

NurturEd Consultants

"Surround yourself with people who are going to lift you higher"

Oprah

nurturedconsultants.co.uk

Printed in Great Britain
by Amazon